PENGUINS

THE WILDLIFE COLLECTION

Contents

First published in the UK in 2014

© Instinctive Product Development 2014

This edition published by Park Lane Books

www.parklanebooks.com

Printed in China

ISBN: 978-1-906969-84-4

Designed by: BrainWave

Creative Director: Kevin Gardner

Written by: Lisa Hughes

Images courtesy of Corbis and Shutterstock

Introduction

■ **ABOVE: An Emperor chick and adult; these penguins are amongst the largest of the species.**

Penguins are aquatic, flightless birds that live exclusively in the southern hemisphere. Antarctica is home to a few species, where these fascinating birds are highly adapted for life in the water. The majority of species are found in the temperate zone, and the Galapagos penguins live close to the equator. Rather than wings, penguins have evolved dark flippers, which match their outer body color and complement their white plumage to the front. The Emperor penguin is the largest species and can grow to around 1.1m or 3 feet 11 inches. The Little Blue is the smallest penguin and is sometimes known as the Fairy penguin, measuring up to 40cm or 16 inches. The larger species tend to inhabit colder regions and the smallest are found in temperate regions.

They are expert "fishermen" who feed on fish, squid, krill (a shrimp-like crustacean), and other sea creatures while they swim underwater. About half their time is spent in the sea, while the other half is spent on land. With their rounded bodies, which come to a point at either end, penguins are highly adapted for swimming. These "fine-tuned" swimmers use their powerful flippers (wings) to propel themselves through water, while their short legs and webbed feet act as a rudder. Built with solid bones – unlike other birds who have lighter bone density for flight – penguins use this to their advantage and are able to dive to 30-60 feet while

hunting for food, although some species (Little Blue, African, Rockhopper) can dive to around 160 feet if necessary, and others can reach around 1,000 feet. These fascinating birds can break through the surface of the water and "fly" (porpoising) through the air before diving back under at speeds of 15 miles per hour or so. Penguins swim rather than fly (they simply don't need the ability to fly, and their bone density and blubber means they are unable to create enough energy to take off), which is vital for hunting. Their wings are small, giving them lower drag and greater agility underwater. The wing bones are fused straight to make them rigid and powerful like a flipper. Penguins also have higher levels of myoglobin (oxygen per body mass) than birds able to fly, and feathers optimized for their environment.

Penguins have around 80 feathers per square inch, enabling them to retain body heat and stay dry as each feather has a fluffy down at the base of it trapping air close to the skin. To counteract this, penguins can fluff their feathers to release air if they become too hot. Feathers overlap and become stiff and small at the tip – keeping them dry underwater by keeping water away from the skin – creating a smooth surface and reducing drag underwater. Molting takes place each year during a two- to three-week period. This encourages healthy feathers all-year-round and grooming is extremely important. While penguins find their short legs and webbed feet particularly helpful in water, it does tend to inhibit them

more on land, but this time is spent preening – for hours at a time – to condition the feathers through the release of an oil found in a gland at the base of the tail. Tails are wedged-shaped and short for most species. Brush-tailed penguins, such as Chinstrap, Gentoo, and Adelie, have around 18 tail feathers, which they also use as a "prop" on land. Vocalization in penguins is extremely important in communicating with mates. Hearing is thought to be good, as is smell, but there have been few studies into penguins' sense of taste. Vision is exceptionally good – both on land and underwater – and the cornea can change shape to adapt to whichever environment the bird is in. Penguins have a "third eyelid" known as a nictitating membrane to protect eyes from injury, and glands beneath the skin above the eyes ensure that excess salt from the ocean is filtered out. As the salt moves on to the beak, penguins are able to shake it off with an action that is much like a sneeze. Penguins don't possess teeth, so food is swallowed whole. Their beaks are powerful, hooked, and designed for hunting, while their rough tongues enable them to hold onto their prey and swallow between five and 10 fish each day. A diet of krill and squid makes for potent guano (excrement).

Depending on the species, of which there are 17, eggs differ in size and shape. It is not easy to distinguish between male and female penguins and experts rely on mating behavior observations, examinations, and DNA analysis.

7

■ **OPPOSITE:** King penguins are pictured beside the water, in which they spend half of their time.

■ **BELOW:** A group of King penguins swim near a melting glacier at Gold Harbor, Southern Ocean, Antarctic Convergence, South Georgia Island.

Evolution

The evolution of penguins stretches back more than 60 million years. Believed to be the decedents of early birds, these interesting species have adapted, over time, for an aquatic environment. Fossils and the studies of penguins have given scientists insight into how penguins evolved into the birds that live on the planet today. Scientists believe that penguins evolved from birds that could fly, but had to adapt to their environment in order to survive. The bones of the wings began to fuse – enabling swimming but rendering flight impossible. This evolution is thought to have taken an extremely long time to develop. This led to their wings, in effect, becoming flippers, and hunting in the oceans of the southern hemisphere became paramount for survival. This ability to evolve is what probably saved penguins from extinction. However, there are theories to suggest that penguin ancestors never did fly, and that penguins have, in fact, always been flightless. There are no fossils to confirm that penguins could fly originally. It appears that basal, or early penguins, probably did not fly, and that scientific research remains speculative.

A large number of penguin species have developed layers of fat (or blubber), especially where populations have been forced to remain in cold and icy climates – evolution is thought to be responsible for this. It is possible, in the past, that these birds would have migrated to warmer climes, but over time penguins stayed within certain parameters; being able to survive harsh conditions would have required additional insulation. Credible theories and research exist about penguin evolution, but some experts cite that penguins have changed so dramatically that they shouldn't perhaps be classified as birds at all. However, the fact that they are unable to fly hasn't been enough to change their classification to date. Studies into penguins and their evolution are ongoing, and DNA analysis has shown that, at one time, there were at least 40 other species of penguins alongside the 17 that are recognized today. It is believed that these birds did not evolve and were unable to survive their environments.

Research shows that during the Cretaceous-Paleogene extinction event (around 66 million years ago when more than three quarters of animal and plant life on Earth were destroyed), basal penguins (the first of the species) were found around the southern areas of New Zealand and some regions of Antarctica. Around this time, these areas were roughly 930 miles apart, rather than the 2,500 miles that separate them today. The time marked the end of the Cretaceous period and it is believed that penguins were not entirely flightless. Early fossils show that species were not equipped for aquatic life in the way that penguins are in the 21st century, but they were probably loon-like (aquatic diving birds), capable of deep diving. Scientists understand that around 38 million years

■ ABOVE: Fossils and skeletons of penguins have given scientists clues as to how these amazing birds have evolved.

9

■ **ABOVE:** Adelie penguin rookeries dot the slopes of Mount Flora, which also contains extensive fossil deposits, Hop Bay, Antarctica.

ago, early species, which did evolve from the basal penguins, had found their way to South America. It is known that giant penguins existed around 30-40 million years ago (growing up to 6 feet or 1.8 meters). Two species have been found in fossil remains around New Zealand, where one was also discovered in the Antarctic. Medium to huge penguins existed around the Antarctic roughly 35 millions years ago – it is thought there were up to 10 different species – while another giant penguin was found much further north in Peru. Giant

penguins disappeared around 25 million years ago, and it is generally agreed that competition for food alongside whales brought about their demise. By this time, smaller penguins were found around the southern regions of South America, the Antarctic, and Australasia.

Fossil evidence remains sparse, with, as stated, no intermediate species between a flying bird and the flightless penguin, but the closest flying relatives of these birds today include the Albatross, Petrels, Shearwaters, and the Gaviidae

■ **ABOVE:** **A painting of the now extinct Great Auk.** (© Allan Brooks/National Geographic Society/Corbis)

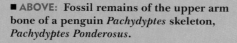

■ **ABOVE:** Fossil remains of the upper arm
bone of a penguin *Pachydyptes* skeleton,
Pachydyptes Ponderosus.

■ **RIGHT:** A group of King penguins walk in
single file.

(a diving bird). To imagine what a "flying penguin" may have looked like, puffins and auks possibly provide some kind of answer, while the Great Auk, which became extinct around 200 years ago, was often mistaken for a penguin. This bird, like the penguin, evolved to increase its swimming ability and eventually became flightless. When the Antarctic continent became completely surrounded by ocean around 200 million years ago, the cold currents in the southern ocean and the formation of the polar ice cap made the waters a rich food source. Birds that could adapt to exploit this resource and breed on remote islands (without fear of land predators) could thrive. Penguin species, according to scientists, specialized in different food sources and only faced decline if

food sources were depleted through competition with other hunters. It is understood that alongside sharks, penguins probably dominated the southern oceans for several million years. Whales and dolphins became rivals for food around 50 million years ago, and in some cases, predators of penguins themselves. Although not taken seriously in the scientific world today, in the 1930s it was suggested that penguins evolved before birds ever took flight. Penguin evolution is studied through chance finds of fossils, more often than not found on remote islands. The fact that penguin fossils are sparse is no great surprise, given that these birds are marine animals. Fossil finds are contained within most of the regions where penguins are found in the modern day, suggesting

that their habitats and range have changed little over millions of years. Fossils indicate that penguins have lived for around 40 million years in the southern regions of the southern hemisphere, and around 23 species are recognized as extinct. Many fossils found are of leg bones – it is suggested that these fossilize most easily – so scientists have had to estimate the sizes of these birds. The dense bones of penguins also aid in counteracting buoyancy. Between three and a half and five and half million years ago, *Pygocelis tyreei* and *Aptenodytes redgeni* species could be found around New Zealand. It is recognized that these are the only two extinct penguin species that belong to the six genera of modern-day penguins, which suggests that more extinct birds – not yet found –

did exist. Penguins are a fascinating example of evolution. Penguin fossils show that these birds belong to the order of Spheniscidae, which includes all penguins whether living or extinct. There are still many unknown elements of penguin evolution, even though substantial information has already been discovered. Evidence does suggest that penguins were, once, not a large part of aquatic life, but what changed this specifically is unclear. Coloration of some species does appear to have occurred dependent on their habitat – research shows that changes in geography and temperatures have helped with the evolution of penguins. It is also suggested that further DNA analysis and research may indicate that there are further species among those already identified.

Species

■ **ABOVE:** **Adelie penguins on an ice flow off Paulet Island. Adelies are one of only two species of penguin found on the Antarctic mainland.**

There are 17 species of penguins at the current time, with the Emperor penguin known as the largest and the Little Blue (Fairy) as the smallest. However, the extant number of species remains under debate, and there are discussions about whether further species exist. All penguins come from the sub-family Spheniscindae, but the White-flippered penguin is sometimes referred to as a separate Eudyptula species, although the majority of experts consider it a subspecies of the Little Blue penguin. (The inclusion of further species will take a great deal of time to materialize, if at all.) Weighing around 3.3 pounds and standing around 12 inches tall, the White-flippered penguin is quite often described as a color morph of the Little Blue. Found to breed only on Motunau Island, near Christchurch, New Zealand, it is named for the white markings on its flippers, unique to this subspecies.

Rockhopper penguins have also caused controversy with regard to species. Traditionally, these crested penguins have been considered one species, however, some cite that there are at least two other species, and classification remains unclear. The Eastern and Southern Rockhoppers are usually referred to as distinct from the Northern Rockhopper, however, some also include the Western Rockhopper. For the purpose of this book, we will refer to the Rockhopper as one species with three subspecies to include the Northern Rockhopper, the Eastern, and the Southern Rockhopper penguins. In addition, another crested penguin, the Royal penguin, is sometimes considered a morph of the Macaroni penguin rather than a species in its own right. Although rare, Royal and Macaroni penguins have been known to mate across species, which has resulted in mixed-species pairs in the wild.

for being timid. The Humboldt has suffered a serious decline over recent decades – conservation of this species is now critical. The King penguin is the second largest of all the species and is gregarious by nature. While the African penguin is known as the Jackass due to its vocalization, the Little Blue is renowned for its huge range of "songs." Macaroni penguins are the largest of the crested species, while the Magellanic are one of the most numerous of the genus Spheniscus. Rockhoppers are named for the way they hop around steep rocky terrain. The Royal penguin has a white face and throat – the only penguin that does among the crested species. Snares Island penguins are the only species that roosts in low trees, while the Yellow-eyed penguin seeks out sheltered nests. Renowned for being reclusive, breeding can be seriously interrupted if a nesting pair are even within sight of any other penguins. Facts for these 17 species are outlined over the next five pages.

The traditional 17 species include the Adelie, African, Chinstrap, Emperor, Erect crested, Fiordland, Galapagos, Gentoo, Humboldt, King, Little Blue, Macaroni, Magellanic, Rockhopper, Royal, Snares Island, and Yellow-eyed penguins. The Adelie, alongside the Emperor penguin, is restricted to the waters around Antarctica, while the African penguin burrows from the hot sun (and its predators) and is often known as the Jackass penguin. The Chinstrap is one of the most numerous penguins in the world and belongs to the brush-tailed (also known as stiff-tailed) group. The Emperor survives the harshest weather of any species, while the Galapagos live in tropical climes close to the equator. As the most northerly of all the penguins, it often endures temperatures exceeding 100 degrees. Crested species all have yellow head feathers, including the Erect crested penguins and the Fiordland, which are also considered the most rare and timid. Gentoo penguins, like the Adelie and Chinstrap, are a brush-tailed species, and are also renowned

■ **ABOVE LEFT: A flock of Rockhopper penguins hop from rock to rock in the Falkland Islands.**
■ **BELOW: A Humboldt penguin nesting in a rock burrow on Tilgo Island, La Serena, Chile.**

Adelie penguin –
Pygoscelis adeliae

Height: 18-24 inches
Weight: 8-10 pounds
Habitat: Antarctic continent within the limits of pack ice
Population: estimated at 4,931,600 (lower risk)

Chinstrap penguin –
Pygoscelis Antarctica

Height: 28-30 inches
Weight: 8.5-9.5 pounds
Habitat: Circumpolar; breeding south of the Antarctic convergence on the Antarctic peninsula and surrounding islands
Population: estimated at 15,000,000 (lower risk)

17

African penguin –
Spheniscus demersus

Height: 25-27 inches
Weight: 6-8 pounds
Habitat: South Africa and Namibia
Population: estimated at 180,000 adults (vulnerable)

Emperor penguin –
Aptenodytes forsteri

Height: 36-44 inches
Weight: 60-90 pounds
Habitat: Circumpolar and marine; within the Antarctic mainly on fast ice in large colonies
Population: estimated at 436,200 (lower risk)

Erect crested penguin – *Eudyptes sclateri*

Height: 25 inches
Weight: 6-7.7 pounds
Habitat: New Zealand (north and south islands), Antipodes, Bounty, and Auckland Islands
Population: estimated at 330,000 (vulnerable)

Galapagos penguin – *Spheniscus mendiculus*

Height: 21 inches
Weight: 5-6 pounds
Habitat: Galapagos Islands of Fernandina and Isabela (600 miles west of Ecuador)
Population: estimated at 3,000-8,000 (endangered)

Fiordland penguin – *Eudyptes pachyrhynchus*

Height: 24 inches
Weight: 6-7 pounds
Habitat: New Zealand and sub-Antarctic islands
Population: estimated at 5,000-6,000 (vulnerable)

Gentoo penguin – *Pygoscelis papua*

Height: 30-35 inches
Weight: 10-14 pounds
Habitat: Antarctic peninsula and sub-Antarctic islands
Population: estimated at 628,000 (lower risk)

Humboldt penguin – *Spheniscus humboldti*

Height: 18-24 inches
Weight: 6-11 pounds
Habitat: Peru and Chile on the western coast of South America
Population: estimated at 13,000 (vulnerable)

King penguin – *Aptenodytes patagonicus*

Height: 37 inches
Weight: 30-45 pounds
Habitat: sub-Antarctic and Antarctic islands
Population: estimated at 3,276,890 (lower risk)

Little Blue penguin – *Eudyptula minor*

Height: 10-12 inches
Weight: 2-3 pounds
Habitat: New Zealand and Australia
Population: estimated at 700,000-1,200,000 (stable)

Macaroni penguin – *Eudyptes chrysolophus*

Height: 28 inches
Weight: 9-13 pounds
Habitat: sub-Antarctic islands close to the Antarctic convergence in the South Atlantic and Indian oceans. Breeding only on the Antarctic peninsula. Spends 75 per cent of time in the sea
Population: estimated at 18,000,000-23,000,000 (vulnerable – due to rapid decline in numbers since the 1970s)

Rockhopper penguin – *Eudyptes chrysocome*

Height: 18-23 inches
Weight: 4.5-8 pounds
Habitat: the rocky islands of the sub-Antarctic and south temperate regions of the Indian and South Atlantic oceans
Population: Northern Rockhopper estimated at 700,000 adults (vulnerable); Southern Rockhopper estimated at 950,000 adults (vulnerable); Eastern Rockhopper estimated at 1,664,000 adults (vulnerable)

Magellanic penguin – *Spheniscus magellanicus*

Height: 14-22 inches
Weight: 7-15 pounds
Habitat: South America (central Chile and Argentina, and further south to the Falkland Islands and Cape Horn)
Population: estimated at 2,600,000 (lower risk)

Royal penguin – *Eudyptes schlegeli*

Height: 26 inches
Weight: 12 pounds
Habitat: Macquarie Island (off New Zealand) and surrounding areas with winters spent in sub-Antarctic waters
Population: estimated at 1,700,000 (vulnerable)

Snares Island penguin – *Eudyptes robustus*

Height: 25 inches
Weight: 6-7 pounds
Habitat: Snares Island chain (New Zealand), although non-breeding range stretches to islands in the Pacific
Population: estimated at 46,000 (vulnerable)

Yellow-eyed penguin – *Megadyptes antipodes*

Height: 21 inches
Weight: 11.5-13 pounds
Habitat: New Zealand (South Island on the southeast coast – including Stewart, Campbell, and Auckland Islands)
Population: estimated at 4,000 to 7,000 (vulnerable due to a 45 per cent decline since the 1970s)

Habitat

Habitats are diverse across penguin species. While some live in extremely cold climates and relatively harsh conditions, there are those that live in much warmer climes. Antarctica is a harsh environment (penguins here nest on ice packs) where many animals and birds would fail to survive, but penguins have adapted to this cold climate. The Galapagos penguins live in the temperate climes of the Galapagos Islands, from which they take their name. Habitats and distribution of penguin species are widespread due to their adaptability. Carl Bergmann, a 19th-century German biologist, proposed the principle that there was a correlation between the ratio of the body surface to weight in warm-blooded animals, meaning that birds and mammals found in cold regions were larger than the same species in warm climates. This principle is recognized in zoology as Bergmann's Rule, and it arguably applies to penguins when discussing different habitats and sizes of species. At higher latitudes larger-sized penguins can be found, while in lower latitudes penguin species are significantly smaller. Penguins, as seen, live in the southern hemisphere (when in the wild) around South America, South Africa, Antarctica, Australia, and New Zealand. All live close to water, and many live on remote islands. All penguins spend time on land and in water, but nests are built on land in which to lay eggs. Time on land, depending on the species, does vary. Some only spend a quarter of their time out of the water, especially when food sources are scarce and hunting is of paramount importance. Habitats need to offer enough

■ **ABOVE:** A typical Galapagos Islands habitat, Ecuador.

■ **BELOW:** A massive penguin rookery has been established on a rocky beach in the South Shetland Islands. The penguins feed primarily on Antarctic krill in the Southern Ocean.

23

food so that fat reserves can be built and maintained. If habitats have natural food sources that begin to decline then penguins are known to migrate. They leave the relative safety of their rookeries and descend on coastal waters that can offer them an alternative food source. Distances traveled may be extensive. Three species known to migrate great distances between breeding and feeding grounds include the Emperor, Humboldt, and Magellanic penguins.

Penguins are particularly social by nature and form colonies where a hierarchy exists. Within this numerous sub-orders are found, and males and females can be found working alongside each other in order to hunt for food or care for young. The environment in which penguins reside plays a huge role in their survival. Habitats are generally found in remote continental regions free from land predators, where the inability to fly is not detrimental to survival. Penguins are usually found near cold-water currents where nutrient-rich food sources are abundant. Although they may return to where they were hatched, to molt and breed, young birds often travel thousands of miles when they first leave their colonies. Colonies of penguins are found on each of the continents in the southern hemisphere. While food in the oceans is vital, penguins also utilize the resources on land. Sticks, rocks, grass, and other natural resources are used to make nests and build burrows. Scientists, however, have been able to establish that penguin habitats have changed over the past 100 years. Much of this is due to global warming – which continues to threaten essential habitats – both in terms of loss of environment and the penguins' ability to travel to breeding grounds some distance away. Where the sun is now hotter, natural habits are affected and penguins struggle to keep themselves cool enough. A large number of old and young birds die due to the strength of the sun, and food sources are greatly depleted too. Changes in habitat can also affect how long a penguin is away searching for food – which in

■ **ABOVE LEFT:** A Gentoo penguin greets its mate as it guards its nest, Antarctica.

■ **ABOVE:** Penguins like to form colonies where a clear and definite hierarchy exists.

turn has a detrimental affect on breeding, rearing young, and mates (who eventually are forced to abandon eggs in order to search for food themselves). Humans also have a detrimental impact on penguin habitats. Where terrain no longer remains natural, penguins struggle to compete with man for space and resources.

Rockhopper penguins live on rocky shorelines where they build nests in high grasses called tussocks. Here they also make burrows. Southern Rockhoppers inhabit regions around South America, where they breed on the Falkland Islands, southern Chile, and southern Argentina. Eastern Rockhoppers (a subdivision of the Southern Rockhopper) make their home on Prince Edward Island, the Crozet Islands, and Kerguelen Islands in the French Southern Territories, and the Marion Islands in South Africa. They also breed on the Heard and Macquarie Islands off Australia as well as the Antipodes

■ **ABOVE:** A Magellanic penguin looks out of its burrow and preens its feathers.

■ **RIGHT:** Emperor penguins form a huddle against the cold temperatures.

Islands, and other islands around New Zealand. Northern Rockhopper penguins breed in the southern Atlantic Ocean on Gough Island and Tristan da Cunha, and in the St. Paul Islands in the Indian Ocean. After leaving their breeding colonies in late summer or early fall, this species spend around five months at sea foraging for food.

The Emperor penguin endures the harshest weather imaginable in order to breed. This species fasts for months through tough winters, relying on fat stores which become stored energy. However, the Emperor penguin's habitat is under serious threat from global warming. They huddle together in wind chills that can reach minus 76 degrees Fahrenheit (60 degrees Celsius), on the Antarctic ice, to conserve warmth. This co-operative behavior sees this species taking turns to inhabit the warmer interior provided by huddling together. Pack ice in the Antarctic is often seen floating in huge pieces, formed in the winter months when the seas surrounding the continent freeze. Mountains here are covered by an ice sheet, miles thick, and more than 98 per cent of Antarctica is covered in ice, leaving just less than two per cent as bare rock. As well as penguins, whales, seals, and albatross all compete for survival. Like the Emperor penguin, King penguins live in Antarctica, although they inhabit the more temperate islands north of the continent. Despite the slightly higher temperatures, King penguins have four layers of feathers and also huddle together for warmth.

Galapagos penguins have a completely different environment where large amounts of time are spent in the

sea to keep cool. Prior to breeding, this species molts and the sea is avoided – unless feeding is essential. When Galapagos penguins spend time on land, they hold their flippers away from the body to maximize heat loss. They are mainly found on Fernandina Island, and the west coast of Isabella Island, although smaller colonies may be found on other remote islands of the archipelago.

Found around the warm waters of Australia, Tasmania, and New Zealand, the Little Blue penguin is not endangered, although threats within its habitat include dogs, foxes, and even ferrets. Large gulls also seriously compromise the species, as do sharks, killer whales, and seals. Endemic to New Zealand, inhabiting the southeast coast of the South Island, Auckland, and Campbell Islands, as well as Stewart Island and the Foveaux Strait, is the habitat of the Yellow-eyed

penguin. The species favors the coastal forest and mixed-species scrub on slopes; however, the loss of coastal forest in recent times has seen the bird adapt to scrub remnants on the South Island. While adult birds remain sedentary, young penguins (or juveniles) disperse from breeding grounds to as far north as the Cook Strait. The Yellow-eyed penguin is threatened by global warming, as are other penguins, where changes in sea temperature have seriously depleted food sources. In addition, introduced mammals in natural habitat have seen chick mortality rates rise through predation.

■ **RIGHT:** Little Blue penguin pioneers arrive on the beach in front of the Twelve Apostles sea stacks, Port Campbell, Victoria, Australia.

Vocalization and Communication

■ **ABOVE: A King penguin calling, King Edward Point, South Georgia Island.**

Penguins are naturally vocal animals, and communication is key to the success of colony populations and mating couples. Penguin calls – or vocalizations – are individually identifiable. Mates are able to recognize each other and their chick. This is crucial in a large colony where these birds are almost indistinguishable by sight. Male and female Emperor penguins have different calls – which are probably different because of courtship rituals and mate selection. The three main penguin

calls include the contact call, the display call, and the threat call. The first, the contact call, helps establish recognition within colonies. The calls of male Emperor and King penguins can be heard more than half a mile away. The display call is rather more complex and is used between mating pairs. The purpose of this call is to convey information on an individual, sexual, and territorial basis. The third vocalization, the threat call, is perhaps the simplest of calls used for warning colony members of predators as well as for defending territory. Alongside vocalizations, penguins are renowned for their physical behaviors, known as displays. Vocalizations and displays combined help to establish communication with regard to nesting territories, mating rituals, nest relief rituals, partner and chick recognition, as well as defense against outside threats.

Each penguin has a distinct call, although these become more complex between mating penguins. The display vocalizations include male penguins' trumpet calls and the swinging of their heads to communicate the claiming of territory over a particular nesting site. The mating couples also vocalize to communicate their pairing both to each other and other members of the colony. These particular calls last throughout the entire breeding season. Chicks have a feeding call – they plead to all adults for food but parents recognize their own chick's vocalizations. As chicks stay together in a "crèche" or nursery while their parents are away foraging for food, this call is particularly important, for both the returning parent and the chick. Physical displays as a form of vocalizing are also incredibly important for penguins. In this way, individual birds can show submissive, defensive, or aggressive behaviors. They wave their heads or flippers to ward off others from their territory, but they bow their heads in submission. Bonding is strengthened through the crucial act of preening (particularly between mating pairs) which helps to maintain feathers and keep them waterproof. While the sense of smell isn't thought to be highly developed

in penguins, it is known to be important in finding their own mate after feeding at sea. Smell is also used to return to the same nesting site year on year. Close relatives can also be identified by smell, according to researchers at the University of Chicago and the Chicago Zoological Society. It is cited that this smell recognition prevents inbreeding and could also lead to penguins finding a mate for a subsequent breeding season.

From a young age, penguins vocalize in order to communicate, although this doesn't tend to happen while they are swimming or diving for food. In addition to vocalizing, penguins will use postures to communicate their intentions. Threat postures are quite common. The penguin will slick the feathers close to its eye and eyelids in order to increase the white area of the eye as this is more threatening to other penguins. Other threat postures – which can be found in many species – include ritualized movements. These may include loud calls, standoff poses, bowing, moving the head up and down, circling, and violent wing flapping. Territory is usually the main issue when it comes to threat poses. Penguin vocalizations are unique in tone, frequency, and beat. Vocalizations of the African penguin include a donkey-like bray, honk, and growl, hence the Jackass tag. The Little Blue penguin is known to make a victory call. This species, despite its small size, is a great defender of territory, and physical displays and threat poses are common. The winner of any dispute gives a triumph display and vocalizes a "victory" bray, described as a distinctive squawk. This not only heralds the winner, but it gives other penguins within the colony a warning: stay away. This highly social species are particularly vocal, and researchers found that Little Blue males had raised heartbeats when played the triumphant calls of a winning territorial male. The measured heartbeats were significantly less when the vocalizations of the loser were played to the same study group of penguins.

31

■ **LEFT:** **Macaroni penguins preening on South Georgia Island.**

Diet and Foraging

■ **ABOVE: A Gentoo penguin parent returns from a successful foraging trip and regurgitates fish for its two-week-old chicks.**

The entire population of penguins consumes around 20-25 million tons of fish, krill, squid, and crustaceans annually (compared to 70 million tons fished by commercial fisheries). They are undoubtedly one of the top predators of the southern hemisphere's oceans. Foraging takes place both inshore and offshore, across a 31-mile range, meaning that there is heated competition for food in localized areas. Breeding colonies rely heavily on rich food sources, and a

■ **LEFT:** Antarctic krill is part of the penguin's diet.
■ **OPPOSITE:** A King penguin feeding a chick, St. Andrews Bay, South Georgia Island, Polar Regions.

significant depletion in supplies has a serious and adverse affect on rearing chicks. The abundance of food is vital to the overall survival of penguins, and while reluctant to halt activities in the interests of wildlife preservation, many fisheries do reschedule fishing trips, or establish exclusion zones in order to make life more bearable for penguins. Fishing during or prior to the breeding season (as happened in the Falkland Islands) has a severely detrimental affect on penguin populations, but putting some measures in place can greatly benefit penguin species while not drastically damaging the economy.

Penguins eat far more than they actually need as they have long periods of fasting. This takes place during the molting season where they need to remain onshore while their new feathers develop. Other fasting times occur during certain periods of the mating season and when the young chicks have hatched. Some fasting penguins – where energy is stored up within the body – go through the entire mating season (courtship, nesting, and incubation) without food. Chicks also fast – around the time they molt and are ready to shed juvenile plumage for adult feathers. By this time they are generally not being fed by their parents so growing stops, but resumes once the molt is complete.

Krill, squid, and various fish make up the penguin diet, and preferences across species are common. This helps to reduce competition for food among species. Smaller penguin species of the Antarctic and sub-Antarctic enjoy krill and squid, while species further north prefer various kinds of fish. Adelie penguins hunt for small krill, Chinstraps prey on large krill, while Emperor and King penguins primarily feed on squid and fishes. Intake does vary from region to region depending on the time of year, but a colony of around five million Adelie penguins can consume 17.6 million pounds of small fish per day. Penguins rely on their good vision for hunting, so scientists are not entirely sure how they manage to forage in the dark or at great depths.

Studies of penguin diet and foraging habits have been conducted on each species. Some scientists found while studying Adelie penguins that diet differed among colonies only slightly. During years where there was little pack ice present in Antarctica, fish was the staple diet, while krill made up the remainder of the food source. Scientists established that when pack ice was heavy, krill were the predominant diet, particularly juvenile krill. Adult krill were only selected when the pack ice was sparse (suggesting that their own breeding was less successful during these times). As trip durations increased (around two days) for foraging, careful studies carried out in the mid-1990s, showed that the amount of food brought to chicks increased, but when foraging for food lasted up to four days the food decreased. It became evident to the study group that food was used for self-maintenance during longer foraging trips, and when foraging was at its most intense the success of feeding the chicks depended on the proximity of the pack ice to the nesting colonies. Further studies in the mid-1990s concluded that krill were scarce in the Antarctic at the time and that penguins had to rely on a smaller prey (a smaller *Euphausiid*), which provided much less energy per bite than the favored krill. This increased foraging times, and at some points both parents were observed leaving the chicks while they both foraged – this was unheard of until the mid-1990s as far as the scientific world was concerned. It ultimately suggested a severe level of desperation within colonies for survival.

Penguins are also known to eat salps, which are larger than krill although they hold a higher percentage of water (hence the preference for krill which provide more long-term energy). Salps are not as economical for penguins as krill, but they do offer an alternative when the favored food is in short supply. Foraging, however desperate, is still limited. Parents need time to find prey, feed themselves, and to fill their stomachs so they can feed their young.

Anatomy

■ **ABOVE:** **King Penguins swimming underwater show their torpedo shape.**

The anatomy of a penguin is fascinating, with its torpedo shape designed for "flight" underwater. Their bodies look rather cumbersome on land, but this adds to their charm and proves just how aerodynamic they are in the sea. Their wings have developed as flippers to aid movement in water, while their bodies are well insulated to help keep cold water away from the skin.

On land, the flippers and tail are used to help penguins maintain balance, but their smooth feathers on their bellies allow them to slide on snow, providing a much faster way to travel. As a result, less energy is used than "waddling" and speed is much more manageable. The main body of each species is predominantly black and white, which helps with camouflage in water – the black on the back of each penguin helps protect them from predators above, while the white belly disguises them from predators below. Each species has a

different bill, or beak, and most are long and thin for catching prey. For the species that mainly favor krill, the beak is shorter and wider. However, all penguins have rough tongues that enable them to hold on to their prey, while the rear-facing spines in their mouths allow them to swallow live catches. The nasal passages are designed to filter out excess salt from seawater. By feeding in the sea, penguins do not need to drink water, as they take it in through swimming. Being able to rid themselves of excess salt is vital. The anatomy of penguins is designed to enable them to survive in their natural habitats – hence the differences across species in terms of height and weight. The head of a penguin – out of water – may look disproportionately large, but in the water this proves an advantage. The head also contains two holes that act a little bit like ears. Bodies are long, while flippers contain flat dense bones that are fused between the elbow and wrist. The feet

species has special adaptations that make them unique from other animals – and even birds. The sternum, for example, is unusually large. This is because penguins require powerful pectoral muscles. (Penguins do actually have knee joints.) Penguins have an unusually long esophagus because their stomach is located low in the body. The stomach is a big muscular bag that has a glandular lining to the top and a folded muscular part at the bottom. It is not uncommon for penguins to swallow small pebbles in order to aid digestion, enabled by the liver and the pancreas. Rapid digestion is avoided by the penguin's ability to adjust the levels of acidity in the stomach, while bacteria is used to prevent food from digesting. Like other mammals penguins have a heart, which pumps blood through the entire body while delivering the necessary oxygen. The oxygen-rich blood circulates through the arteries and this circulation is vital for maintaining body temperature. Birds, including penguins, have no diaphragm, so a constant stream of air passes through several air sacs. Penguins breathe through their abdomens, as the extension of the belly allows the inhalation of air.

Around one in 50,000 penguins is an Isabelline penguin, meaning that it has brown, rather than black, feathers. These birds tend to live for less time than their black-plumaged counterparts. In addition, they are often rejected as mates and do not have as much protective camouflage as other penguins of the same species. All species contain Isabelline penguins.

and legs are set back from the rest of the body, which also enables penguins to walk upright. Penguins are able to hop and jump when they need to travel through rocky terrain – hence the name Rockhopper for example – and their stiff webbed feet include four toes attached to strong, short legs. Claws feature under the bottom of the feet.

The eye is one of the most dramatic features of the penguin – whichever the species. The eyes have evolved with a flattened cornea, enabling clear sight both above and below water. Each eye contains main blood vessels in the cornea, which stops the eye from freezing by warming it. The nictitating membrane also moves back and forth horizontally to further protect the eye from freezing seawater. Each

■ **ABOVE:** Penguins have very dramatic-looking eyes, as illustrated by this Rockhopper penguin from Argentina.

■ **OPPOSITE:** The Rockhopper penguin's anatomy enables it to hop and jump over uneven terrain.

■ **BELOW:** Penguins can look odd with their large stomachs, but are perfectly built for swimming.

Young

■ **ABOVE:** Emperor penguin parents with their chick, Antarctica.

While male and female penguins care for their young together, for most species the parenting roles are fairly traditional. However, the Emperor penguin changes this stereotypical image where roles are reversed. It is the male Emperor penguin that incubates the egg while the female forages for food. Once the chick hatches, the male produces milk from his esophagus.

Penguins are not sexually dimorphic (male and female penguins look alike), however, during the mating season, it may be possible to tell females from males by the footprints left on the back of the female during mating. Emperor penguins travel up to 70 miles to reach the breeding site

between March and April each year. Eggs are laid between May and early June, after which time the female returns to the sea for two months in order to feed. Incubation of the egg takes around 65 days and is the male's sole responsibility. Females return in mid-July to early August when the egg hatches. The male calls out to the female by lowering his head onto his chest. His mating ritual is both visual and auditory — with a trumpet-like call — in order to attract a female. The Emperor male moves around proudly spreading his flippers while he searches for his mate. When a male and female form a bond, they bow deeply to each other to indicate they are ready to mate. Penguins have no external

■ **ABOVE:** A Gentoo penguin feeds its small chick as another breaks from an egg.
■ **ABOVE RIGHT:** An Emperor penguin male and female greet each other, Antarctic Peninsula.

genitalia and mating takes place through the cloaca (an orifice for urinating, defecating, and reproduction) of each bird being pressed together. In the male, this is where the testes are stored. Once successful and an egg is laid, the female carefully transfers it to her mate without touching the ice (which would cause the egg to freeze and the chick to die). The male then tucks the egg under a large fold of skin until it hatches, while the female returns to the feeding grounds. (During this time the male generally fasts for around two months.) The female finds her mate and chick by listening to the "trumpet" calls of thousands of breeding birds.

Emperor penguins tend to be serially monogamous and remain with their mate for one season at least. If they can't find each other the following breeding season – around 15 per cent do – they have little choice but to find an alternative mate. In the third year, it is estimated that around five per cent of Emperor penguins find each other for the subsequent breeding season. Both the Humboldt and Adelie species also try to remain monogamous for longer than one breeding season. The Adelie penguin will present his prospective mate with a rock – at their feet – to secure commitment. Once the rock is laid at the feet of the female, the two penguins stand belly to belly and perform a mating song. As migratory animals, Adelie penguins travel from the Antarctic pack ice to arrive at their breeding grounds – rookeries – during the fall. Here, nests built from stones piled together are created extremely carefully so as to avoid the temptation of other males trying to take the stones to their own prospective mates. Adelie penguins lay two eggs in around November, which are green or brown in color. Parents share the incubation period, but the female generally returns to the sea before the male. The whole family take to the sea in March.

Of all the penguin species, only the King and Emperor penguins do not build a nest. Nests tend to be a simple pile of stones – like those built by the Adelie penguin – although theft and swapping is rife across species. Nests that do last are built higher than the surrounding land so that if snow melts as temperatures rise, the nest isn't flooded. Like the Emperor, the King penguin keeps the egg on its feet, and the chick when its hatched, covered in a "brood" pouch until the chick

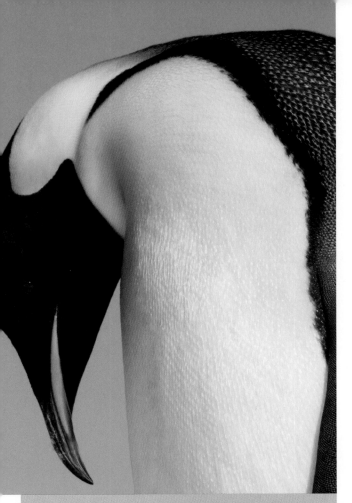

is able to regulate its own temperature.

Breeding colonies are extremely noisy, busy, and smelly. In the past, scientists would walk through these colonies in order to record data. Today, this practice is frowned upon and other ways of monitoring and watching penguins are employed. Nests within colonies are kept just far enough apart so that chicks are unable to reach each other (and damage their neighbors). Breeding colonies may consist of a small number of breeding pairs, or up to half a million breeding pairs. Many species, like the Adelie, lay two eggs, although raising two chicks is rare. If two chicks survive, and food is in short supply, the largest and strongest chick is the only one to receive food. Chicks feed on regurgitated krill and fish and only leave the nest – or their parent's feet – once they are large enough to regulate their own body temperature. Once out of the nest (or the brood pouch), chicks form crèches to keep themselves safe from the elements and predators, including Skuas (seabirds).

■ **BELOW: Emperor penguin chicks in Antarctica.**

Behavior

■ **ABOVE: Adult Gentoo penguins showing aggressive traits, Neko Harbor, Southern Ocean, Polar Regions.**

Penguins express themselves with their bodies, in much the same way that humans have body language. Penguins, however, have a "language" of their own and a whole host of poses, motions, and sounds, which are recognizable to other penguins. Birds in large colonies need to recognize and understand each other. The ethology – or behavioral science – of penguins is complex and has taken scientists many years to understand. This work is still ongoing. Much of the behavior of penguins, as with other animals and birds in the wild, is instinctive survival, but it can broadly be described in four groups. General behavior includes the actions of an individual penguin with regard to support – for example preening, cleaning, bathing, sleeping, feeding,

and body temperature maintenance. The second type of behavior is aggressive or defensive, where penguins compete for mates and nesting territory by physically attacking one another. This behavior can also be used against other animals and predators. Sexual and courtship defines the third type of behavior, which includes attracting mates, and bonding, while the fourth behavior includes breeding. This represents the behaviors between parents, and their chicks. General behavior is the only type that refers to an individual bird because there is no reliance on another bird or the need for any interaction. All other types of behavior involve more than one individual penguin.

Preening is essential for a penguin's survival. The preen

■ **ABOVE:** A Macaroni penguin adult grooming its stiff tail feathers, Cumberland Bay, South Georgia Island.
■ **ABOVE RIGHT:** Emperor penguin chicks panting in the warm spring weather, Riiser-Larsen Ice Shelf, Weddell Sea, Antarctica.
■ **OPPOSITE & NEXT PAGE:** Penguins can sleep standing up or lying on the ground.

gland helps to oil the feathers and ensures they stay waterproof. In colonies, guano is excreted absolutely everywhere, which can make for a significant mess and filthy penguins. Nest building is also a messy business – earth flies everywhere – and penguins usually bathe in the mornings. When penguins leave the water, their first instinct is to clean and preen. Uniform motions are used with the bill to clean feathers. The preen gland, which is a double-sac located near the base of the tail, is utilized after every motion. The bill and head are rubbed over the preen gland before being rubbed over the feathers, flippers, and skin. The preen gland contains a mix of oil and wax, which not only waterproofs the birds but also prevents dehydration and acts against bacteria, algae, and mildew. This behavior often extends into courtship and breeding and is a sign of bonding and commitment.

Warmth and insulation are extremely important for penguins – particularly species in the Antarctic, so huddling is considered a way of showing considerate (and essential) behavior in order to survive. On the other side, the fascinating insulation they possess can see them become too hot, especially under hot sun, so moving the flippers away from the body and panting help to encourage heat loss. Penguins found in warmer climes also have no feathers around the pink parts of their bills, in order to control body temperature.

Penguins can sleep standing up – with their head under a wing – or lying on the ground. Short naps are usual, but they stay alert for dangers. While penguins are at sea they need to sleep, but quite how they manage this is as yet unknown. Sleeping penguins conserve energy by a slowing down of the metabolism. Staring, interestingly, is an important part of behavior for penguins. They are unable to focus through both eyes at the same time, so staring is usually done from the side, or by alternating eyes. This is a warning to another penguin not to come too close. This is a breeding behavior that is designed to protect the nest or chick. Alternating stares tend to be more aggressive and are often accompanied by the bill pointing forward to highlight the seriousness of the situation. Fights using beaks are fairly ferocious and eyes are kept half-closed in case of injury. These fights are common among large colonies where countless breeding pairs are nesting in close proximity. However, utilizing a "slender walk" can help avoid a fight. This is used to bypass the nests and chicks, and territories of other birds. The penguins almost elongate themselves to become taller and thinner, thereby making walking between nests easier and less likely to cause offence. Ecstatic displays during courtship and breeding are engaging. Males and females may call together and they rub their heads and necks against each other in order to further bonding. Just before mating Emperor penguins are known to take a "mutual walk," although other species have been known to do this – particularly around the nest.

All penguins are social animals and all live in colonies. They

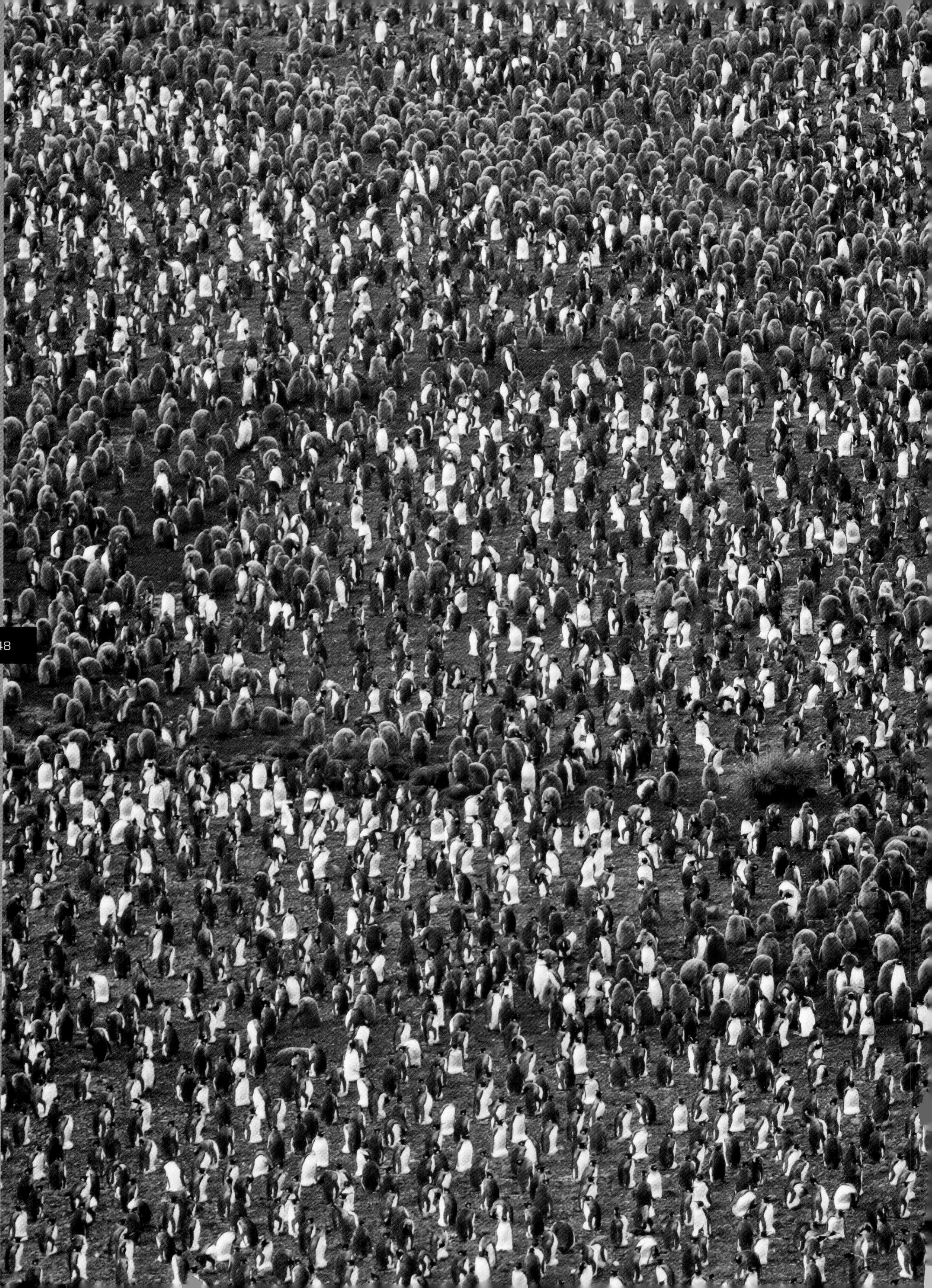

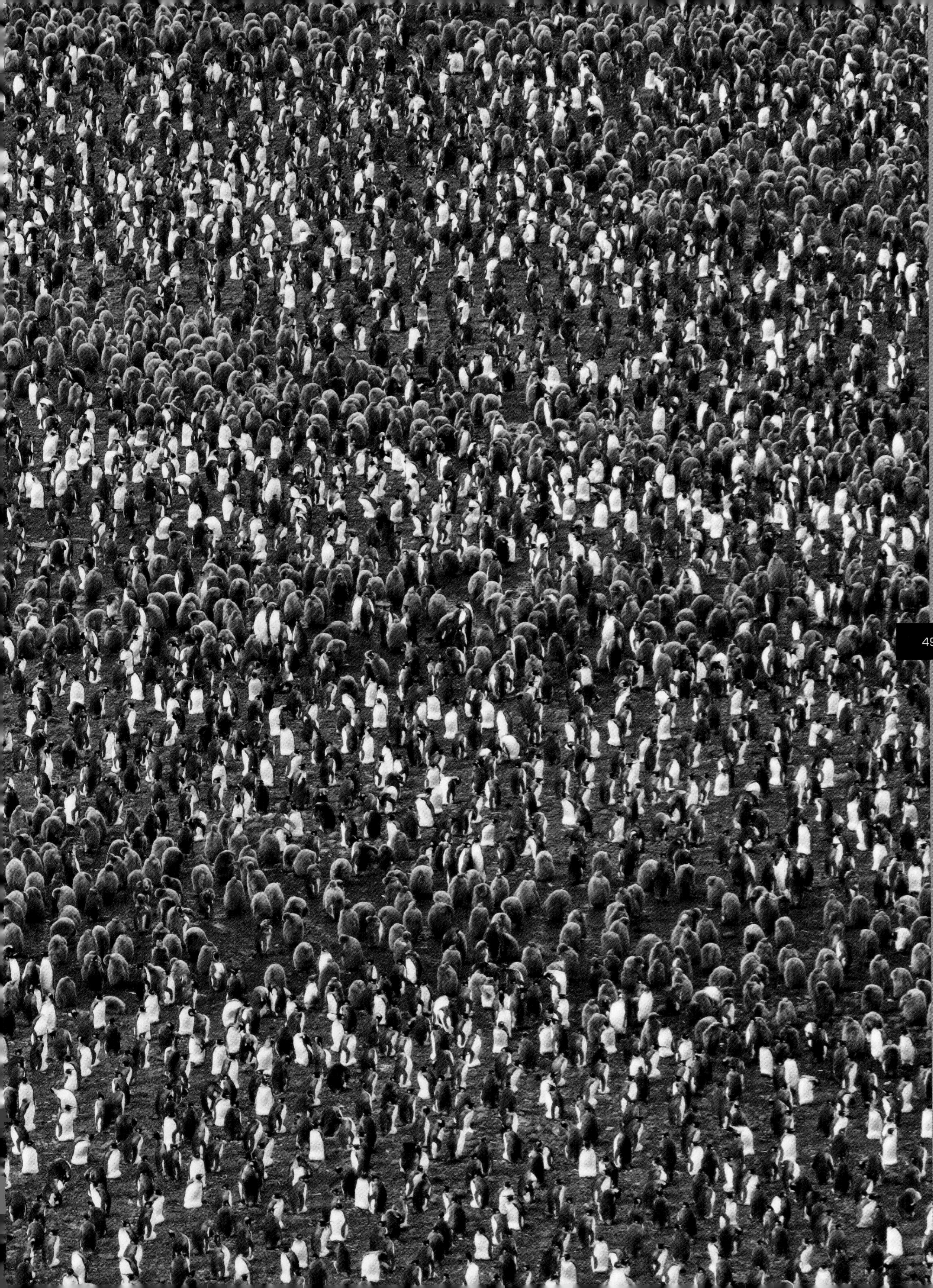

may swim and feed in groups, but they tend to be solitary when diving for food. However, this makes them more vulnerable to predators. Feeding in groups further provides protection. Being part of a huge colony provides safety in numbers – resulting in socializing on a grand scale. Penguins are considered highly intelligent and form strong bonds. They are naturally curious and seemingly crave physical interaction. If a mating pair – who have mated over a number of seasons – are suddenly separated, due to predation for example, the remaining mate is often loath to find an alternative partner. Females that no longer mate can, and do, help with the young of other members of the colony.

Like other penguins, the Adelie species is highly social and forages and nests in groups, although they compete fiercely for nesting sites, especially on higher ground where it's well drained. They are also particularly aggressive toward other penguins that "steal" stones from their nests. King penguins

■ **RIGHT: A Royal penguin pair at rest on the rocky beach, Macquarie Island, Australia.**

■ **BELOW: King penguins can dive to around 771 feet and up to 1,000 feet in a "V" shape when looking for food.**

51

were shown to dive to around 771 feet following studies in the 1970s, and can dive up to 1,000 feet in a "V" shape, where they search for food (around 50 per cent of the dive time) before returning to the surface. It was also proved that King penguins swim around 17 miles to the average foraging site. This species can also porpoise.

In 2012, nearly 100 years after it was written, the report by George Levick, a surgeon and medical officer on Captain Scott's ill-fated 1910-13 Terra Nova expedition, was rediscovered. Levick's report into the "shocking" behavior of Adelie penguins had been described as too graphic in the early 20th century. The four-page pamphlet describes the sexual behaviors of this species, written in 1915. Levick had observed and recorded information on the Adelie colony at Cape Adare, but he was extremely shocked by what he witnessed: sexual coercion, physical abuse of chicks, and what he saw as unacceptable behaviors between unpaired males and females.

The African penguin behavior includes the loud "donkey-like" bray emitted during its ecstatic display. It not only reinforces bonding couples, but is used in the courtship ritual.

■ **RIGHT:** Adelie penguins shocked the medical officer on Captain Scott's Terra Nova expedition with their shocking behavior!

Population

■ **ABOVE:** **The Erect crested penguins at the enormous Orde-Lees Rookery, North Coast, Antipodes Island, New Zealand –**
70 per cent of this species has been lost in the last 20 years.

Of the 17 species of penguins, 13 are considered threatened or endangered, and some species are believed to be on the brink of extinction. Declining populations include the Erect crested penguin which has lost around 70 per cent of its population over the past 20 years. Since the 1970s, the Galapagos penguin has suffered the loss of around 50 per cent of its population. It is estimated that this species is facing a 30 per cent chance of extinction in the 21st century.

■ **LEFT: A Galapagos penguin adult and juveniles, Galapagos Islands, Ecuador.**

■ **OPPOSITE: African penguins at the Table Mountain National Park, Cape Town, South Africa.**

The effects of climate change, overfishing, oil pollution, and predation by introduced mammals are taking their toll. These major factors are widely regarded among penguin biologists across the globe to be the main threat to penguin populations. Held every three to four years, the International Penguin Conference is attended by more than 175 experts and concerned parties, including biologists, government official, conservationists, and aquarium and zoo professionals from more than 20 nations, hoping to make a difference to the plight of falling penguin populations. Across penguin species, populations are in significant decline or under threat from these serious, common factors. Climate change, for many, remains top of the agenda. Many species of penguin are dependent on small schooling fish for food. This includes masses of anchovies, sardines, and other small finfish brought to habitats by cold-water currents. When the El Nino occurs in the Pacific, the sea surface temperature is dramatically warmed, which in turn blocks the cold currents along the western coast of South America. Galapagos and Humboldt penguins, found along the coasts of Peru and Chile, have suffered from food shortages as a result, and it is the young who are most affected. While Galapagos are threatened with chance of extinction, Humboldt penguins have been classified as endangered. They are, unfortunately, not alone. African penguins found in Namibia and South Africa are also classified as endangered. Breeding colonies in the western part of this species' range have routinely disappeared and now that cold-water currents have shifted, food is predominantly found off shore. This means that the distances between feeding and breeding have been greatly increased and, as a result, have had a devastating affect on African penguin populations. It is estimated that by 2100, Emperor penguins will be in significant decline due to pack ice deterioration. It is now imperative that this species adapts to its ever-changing environment and migrates. Two huge icebergs in the Ross Sea in the Antarctic have caused great hardship for Adelie penguins. This huge physical barrier has not only resulted in lower breeding rates, but migration has been virtually impossible. Environmental conditions are unpredictable and penguins' timing with regard to migrating, nesting, mating, and foraging are now more critical than ever.

With overfishing rife throughout many of the southern hemisphere's oceans, Chinstrap and Macaroni penguins have seen anchovy and sardine stocks severely depleted. Add climate change affects on fish stocks, and starvation rates are high. Breeding successes are also lower and disease is contributing to the vulnerability of these populations. Meanwhile, in New Zealand, Yellow-eyed and Fiordland penguins face the real threat of introduced predation. Weasels are a huge threat to penguin populations. For the Rockhopper penguins in the sub-Antarctic, many populations have suffered a 40 per cent decline (and up to 94 per cent in some colonies). Long-term monitoring of penguins in the Antarctic and sub-Antarctic seems to reveal a complex picture with regard to populations. Over the past 30 years, populations of Adelie penguins have fluctuated. Gentoo penguin populations seem to have risen, while Chinstrap penguins have decreased significantly in number. King penguins, on the other hand, have increased in number from a few hundred breeding pairs at the start of the 20th century to nearly half a million today. Many have asked why there are such differences in populations of species. It is widely recognized that food supply and available nest sites are the largest contributing factors – alongside pack or sea ice. Sea ice has reduced by up to 40 per cent in the past 25 years or so, which in turn has impacted on krill nurseries. Long-term research programs continue to provide valuable insight into specific penguin populations and the factors that affect them.

Long-term Survival

Penguins are particularly adaptable creatures, responding to changes within their environment, all be it slowly. However, there are certain limitations, and impacts on the environment play a significant part in the long-term survival of penguin species.

Inshore feeding penguins that rely totally on localized food supplies are particularly vulnerable, and while most spend more than half their lives at sea, accessible stretches of land are still a prerequisite for breeding. In addition, breeding grounds require sustainable food sources for rearing young. While penguins remain resilient and adaptable, their future in today's modern world has never been so fragile. Despite their longevity and ability to "fast" over extended periods

of time, reproduction is slow. Annual survival rates of adults remain high, however, losses in eggs and chick mortality result in fewer additions to populations and the long-term survival of colonies. The fact that penguins live in colonies also poses questions about survival. Young adults do not begin breeding immediately, and depending on the species – Little Blue penguins start breeding at around two to three years of age, while some crested species don't begin breeding until the age of eight – the average age for starting reproduction is more than six years in offshore foraging penguins and around three years of age for inshore foraging birds. This demographic also shows that some "super" pairs breed disproportionately to some other pairs, which fail to breed at all. By default, penguins are slow to respond to population fluctuations, and colonies may be affected as a result. Smaller populations are particularly at risk from environmental changes, which in addition to disappearing food sources, habitats, and an increase in man-made pollutants and increasing numbers of predators, makes long-term survival a crucial issue. To that end, it was decided in the late 1980s to tag the flippers of penguins for scientific study. Known as flipper banding, it was thought that penguin species could be monitored (in much the same way as other species of wild animals and birds). However, in a 10-year study, concluded in 2000, it was actually found that flipper banding had a significant detrimental

■ **ABOVE:** Little Blue penguin chicks in their burrow, Tasmania, Australia.
■ **BELOW:** Emperor penguin biologist Bernard Stonehouse in a colony, Riiser-Larsen Rookery, Weddell Sea, Antarctica.

impact on penguins. The study showed that of the 36,000 penguins who were flipper banded, survival rates dropped by around 16 per cent. King penguins tagged in this way produced up to 39 per cent fewer chicks. Not only did the study raise the question of ethics, but it highlighted that data collected during the research was possibly unsound due to the reactions it caused in the birds involved. It also raised the serious question of long-term survival. A band, made of stainless steel, was placed on an individual bird's flipper to monitor behavior and ecology. It was thought that the bands caused these birds to take longer to swim and to expend more energy; hence they bred later, if at all, having arrived later at colonies. Scientists dubbed this the "drag effect." The cost of flipper banding was undoubtedly increased mortality rates and a significant decrease in reproduction success.

Exploitation of penguins was prevalent in the 19th century and the early part of the 20th century, where eggs, oil, feathers, and meat were all utilized. Rockhopper penguins were even used as bait for crayfish in the south Atlantic. Conservation, regulations, and the Antarctic Treaty (1959) helped change the fate of penguins, although predators and other issues remain a problem. While hunting adult penguins became illegal, it took many years for egg collection to be outlawed. Domesticated and wild animals, particularly dogs, are prone to attacking penguins and continue to pose a serious threat to the long-term survival of these birds.

Today, penguin populations continue to decline steadily due to fishing, pollution, disease, and climate change. In the Antarctic, some species show a continual decline (although in some locations traditionally low numbers are increasing), including Emperor penguins. Overall, despite some increases in species – most notably King penguins on Heard Island, Australia – populations across Antarctica are falling. Understanding why this is happening, and the measures needed to change this decline, will help with long-term survival. Fishing and climate change are having a dire impact on penguins. Disease and pollution are more localized and affecting individual populations. Today, humans compete with penguins for food – krill fishing is a major industry in the Antarctic – but these fish are vital for the region's ecosystem and are a crucial prey for penguins. As the food resources in the Antarctic begin to fall, with trawlers claiming huge catches, a further reduction in krill comes in the form of the sea ice decline. It is no coincidence that the falling numbers of penguins corresponds to withering sea ice and increased fishing activities. Climate change is another terrifying factor; while the past 50 years has seen the global temperature increase by 1 degree, in western Antarctica it has increased by 3 degrees. The sea ice is shrinking, which is affecting a vital breeding ground for penguins in the region, while food resources may be affected differently, and breeding during climate change may not coincide with food resources. This further exacerbates the issues these birds face.

■ **ABOVE: An Adelie penguin group riding a sculpted iceberg, Terre Adelie Land, east Antarctica.**

■ **OPPOSITE: Chinstrap penguins, Deception Island, Antarctica.**

Conservation and Popular Culture

■ **ABOVE:** A penguin affected by fuel oil from a stricken container ship is rubbed down with cooking oil at a wildlife center in the Bay of Plenty, on the east coast of New Zealand's North Island. Cooking oil is one of the liquids used to aid the removal of fuel oil.

All species of penguin are legally protected. As 10 or more of the 17 species are already considered "at risk," it may be a little too late for some colonies of birds. Reauthorized in 1991, the Antarctic Treaty was originally signed by 12 nations to ensure its protection and preservation. Hunting and egg collection were banned, and all specimens must now be approved by, and reported to, the Scientific Committee for Antarctic Research under permit.

Education about the conservation of penguins is vital and, today, aquariums, zoos, institutions, and other organizations play a crucial role in awareness programs. One initiative, launched in April 2013, was the use of satellites in counting penguin populations. Traditionally used for weather patterns, transmission, peacetime movements, and warfare, photographs taken from satellites are now counting individual birds. More than 595,000 Emperor penguins were counted in Antarctica – although there were some issues with regard to which dots were penguins and which were snow – and ground level counts backed up the findings. A specially developed algorithm was used to determine birds from snow, because counting populations from space proved much easier than navigating extensive sea ice where the terrain is

dangerous. It is hoped that this "cost-effective" method will help with penguin conservation for many years to come.

To some extent, penguins are protected in the environments in which they live – remote areas, now protected legally. However, alongside krill fishing, it is believed that pollution affects penguins dramatically, as humans encroach and oceans become clogged with man-made refuse and spillages. In addition, tourism may bring its problems, particularly in populated areas such as South Africa and South America. However, controlled tourism has proved that penguins are largely unaffected by the growth of this industry. Oil spills are completely devastating for penguin populations nesting close to busy shipping lanes. While penguins dive in and out of the water they often face oil spills floating on the surface, as they come up for air, whereby, once they are covered in oil, they lose the ability to protect themselves from the cold. Cleaning themselves can lead to poisoning. Oil finds its way into oceans from illegal dumping to warfare and accidents, but once on the water its affects are devastating for birds and sea life. Sea birds, including penguins, are among the worst casualties of oil spills. Around 40,000 Magellanic penguins are victims of oil pollution along

■ **ABOVE:** A Jackass penguin covered in oil from a spill.

the coast of Argentina annually. As much of the oil spillages are deliberate rather than accidental, many of these deaths could be avoided. Most spillages consist of ballast water – the oily seawater that is used to fill tankers on their way to collect fresh oil – as these ships are designed to operate when fully laden. A large number of tankers do not expel the ballast water in the appropriate environment and this oily water then becomes a significant threat to wildlife. Accidents, however, will continue to happen, despite tighter regulations (which are difficult to enforce), and emergency contingency plans need to allow for rough weather, when most disasters take place. Penguins are particularly susceptible to spillages – many of which take place away from shore – in the modern world, it is believed that many penguins fall victim to unseen spillages happening on a regular basis unnoticed out at sea, which is equally damaging, if not more so, than large-scale one-off disasters. If penguins are spotted coated in oil, rescued, and treated, their survival rate is higher than other seabirds. This is because they have subcuticular fat deposits, which help them avoid hypothermia to some extent, although the treatment of these birds is relatively small-scale, compared with the large numbers that suffer annually.

While penguins can, and do, adapt to their environment to some extent, they are less able to cope when changes occur due to fishing, pollution, and coastal development. Extinction could become a real possibility if measures are not taken to protect these birds. In some regions, penguins are still illegally slaughtered for fishing bait and food. In areas around South America, eggs are still collected. Other, less obvious, threats also arise for some species. Guano deposits – mineral deposits formed from bird droppings in hot climates – are natural burrowing sites for a number of species found around South America and South Africa. These deposits are attractive fertilizers for man, leading to the demise of species such as the Humboldt penguin, where breeding habitats have been destroyed.

Other human activities are also taking their toll. In Australasia, the growth of marinas has brought the Little Blue penguin under threat, while illegal sea-cucumber fishermen, with their makeshift shanties, are seriously affecting Galapagos penguins.

In September 2000, the International Penguin Conservation Work Group was inaugurated by penguin conservationists across the globe. Following the fourth

■ **ABOVE & RIGHT:** *Happy Feet* **and its sequel, along with movies such as** *Mr. Popper's Penguins*, **have reminded the public of why penguins are so likeable and have highlighted interest in conservation and preservation.**

International Penguin Conference, the newly formed group, comprising biologists, aquariums, zoos, international organizations, and research institutes, dedicated itself to the protection and preservation of penguins.

Penguins have enjoyed a place in popular culture since the 2000s due to books, movies, and TV shows, and even online gaming. *Happy Feet, Surf's Up, Madagascar, Mr. Popper's Penguins, Club Penguin*, and other popular media have all contributed to continued and increased popularity of these fascinating birds. Penguins in popular culture are typically depicted as friendly, and while their physical form often highlights a more comical side, they are usually portrayed with great dignity. *Pingu,* shown in 100 short episodes, was created in 1986. The penguins depicted in the *Madagascar* movies are shown as perhaps more sinister and mischievous, however, there is a comical element to their portrayal, where they work as a team. The Penguin in *Batman* is more sinister still. He first appeared on screen in the *Batman* series of the 1960s, where he believed himself to be a "gentleman of crime." However, he made his debut much earlier as one

of Batman's most detested adversaries in 1941 in comic books – which also introduced Batman as a superhero – in a series called *Detective Comics.* Another "poison" penguin featured in *Wallace and Gromit*, the UK animated comedy movie series by Nick Park. Known as Feather McGraw, the penguin "disguises" himself as a chicken (with the aid of a rubber glove), in order to steal a priceless diamond. He finds himself outwitted by the dog "Gromit," the silent, yet highly intelligent "straight-man" to the hapless inventor, "Wallace." In *RuneScape,* an online game, the penguins are devious creatures from Palingrad with a military complex and grand plans for domination. This contrasts somewhat with *Club Penguin*, aimed at a younger gaming audience where cartoon penguins live in a virtual world. Just one year after launching in 2005, *Club Penguin* became the number one game on Miniclip, the largest online game site, and partnered with the Walt Disney Company in 2007 in order to provide unprecedented opportunities for children in a safe online environment.

Companies and other organizations have also used penguins as part of their identity through the use of mascots and logos (including Tux, the Linux Kernel mascot), while politics, and food – the Penguin biscuit – have also used these flightless birds in popular culture. In the US, several pro, minor, college, and high school sports teams are named after penguins, including the Youngstown State Penguins and the Pittsburgh Penguins. These birds are often depicted in popular culture where their striking black and white plumage is shown as a "tuxedo." This was used to great effect in the movie *Mary Poppins* where the animated penguins performed as waiters. In Western culture, if required to dress formally in a tux, it is common to refer to wearing a "penguin suit."

Useful Websites

wwf.org.uk/adopt-a-penguin

www.antarctica.ac.uk

www.penguins.cl/african-penguins

www.birdlife.org/datazone/speciesfactsheet

www.photovolcanica.com/PenguinSpecies/

www.photovolcanica.com/PenguinSpecies/.../EmperorPenguin

www.photovolcanica.com/PenguinSpecies/.../MacaroniPenguin

www.penguin.net

www.seaworld.org/animal-info/info.../penguin

www.birdlife.org.za/conservation/seabirds/tracking-penguins

www.bbc.co.uk/earth/hi/earth_news

www.cityofportsmouth.com/school/dondero/msm/bird

www.arkive.org › Species › Birds

10000birds.com/african-penguins-in-peril

www.pbs.org/wnet/nature/episodes/the-world-of-penguins

www.coolantarctica.com/.../Penguin_royalty_King_and_Emperor

www.gdargaud.net/Antarctica/PenguinFAQ.html

www.patrickdepinguin.com/penguins/

www.birdpark.com.sg/shows-feedings/feeding-times.html

climateclassroomkids.org/.../Activity2_Penguin

www.kidcyber.com.au/topics/penguin.htm

www.natureworldnews.com

www.actionbioscience.org/environment/

libguides.tts.edu.sg

www.enchantedlearning.com/subjects/birds/

www.squidoo.com

www.seabirds.org/news.htm

www.eoearth.org/view/article/155172/

www.penguins-world.com/

a-z-animals.com/animals/african-penguin/

www.penguinscience.com

www.animalfactguide.com

www.nationalgeographic.com

www.zsl.org

www.allaboutbirds.org